BEING BIG AND YET SMALL

Keeping the Magic in a Large Company

Michael R Baer

Being Big and Yet Small

Being Big and Yet Small

INTRODUCTION

We were all small once. We started there. Everyone starts there.

And then you became big. Really big. In the case of my company, we are at least fifteen times bigger than where we started! It doesn't matter how we got here. Acquisitions. Organic growth. Geographic expansion. National Accounts. Specialization. All these roads led to today.

How do you feel about being big? What do you think about all of this? As I talk with people from companies that have leapt from small to big, I hear many different things:

- Some are really excited.
- Some are really scared.
- Some feel lost in the crowd.
- Some see great opportunity.
- Some barely noticed it happened.
- Some don't like the bigger company.
- Some think being large brings greater impact.
- Some long for the good ol' days.
- Some have given up.

The purpose of this short work is to look at the challenges of being big and how to optimize the moment. It's also my purpose to address some of the fear and uncertainty you and your teams may be feeling. I want to think out loud about the idea of being big and yet small at the same time.

So here are some of the questions I'll try to answer:

- How can we be big (and even bigger) and still have the feel of being small?
- How can an individual find his or her way in such a large corporation?
- How can we optimize the power of being large and well-resourced and at the same time keep the nimbleness and hunger of a start-up?

PART ONE
The Problem of Bigness

"I sabotage myself for fear of what bigness could do."
--Alanis Morissette

One of the funniest of Tom Hanks' early movies is *Big*. It's the story of a young boy who makes a wish through a carnival game and ends up being transformed overnight into a grown man. The frustrations and misadventures of being "big" while still being "small" make up the rest of the hilarious story.

In many ways, *Big* is an apt analogy for what has happened with a company that has become huge. Like Tom Hanks' character, you are now living some of the challenges of bigness.

Feeling Disconnected

In *Leaders Eat Last,* Simon Sinek speaks of how tribes work and how companies are much like tribes. One dynamic I gleaned from the book is the Rule of 150. The basic idea is that

Being Big and Yet Small

a person can feel connected to a group and have meaningful relationships within the group until it exceeds about 150 people. After that, friendships become acquaintances and acquaintances become names on org charts and names on org charts become faceless departments.

Personally, I remember a time when I knew virtually every person in my company by name. We were much smaller and I could tell you where most worked and what their title was. In many cases, I could tell you their spouse's name and even their children's names. Not today…although I'm working on it! Many have told me they have similar experiences in their new large company.

It's not surprising that colleagues feel a bit disconnected or lost in the crowd. In one sense, we actually are if the Rule of 150 is accurate.

Things Don't Matter as Much

I'm sure no one imagined that they could run Enron out of business or spend Kodak into oblivion. In big companies, unlike smaller ones, it's hard to imagine that a little less attention on frugality even matters. After all, you now make hundreds of millions; what's a couple of thousand or a few hundred here or there? There must be bank vaults filled with money to cover every expense, every hire, every increase, every purchase, every trip, everything; after all, you're big. It just doesn't seem to matter as much.

In the same way, it would be easy for people in a large company to imagine that there's always "someone else" to fix the problem, to correct their error, to cover their omission. I remember many years ago when I worked in the former Soviet Union. I was speaking with the CFO of a closed tractor plant in Bishkek, Kyrgyzstan and suggesting that he and some of the former managers reopen the plant and run it. This time the investors would be real capitalists instead of their Soviet comrades. "Oh no," Ivan said. "Someone will come. Someone will come and help." That's the thinking that can creep into a big company. There's always "someone" to help, to come.

Systems or Collaboration

There is a brilliant TEDTalk in which mathematician Yves Morieux demonstrates the power of collaboration and true, interdependent teamwork in contrast to mechanical measurements and systems. In particular, he shows how a relay team that is excellent in terms of each individual's contribution but deficient in overall cooperation will actually lose the race to a slower but more collaborative team. *They* forgot that *their* goal was to get *their* baton across the finish line so that *their* team could win.

A few years back, I was speaking with a consultant when he remarked that he wondered how our company got anything done. Specifically, he was criticizing the overlap and fuzziness of our organizational structure. I laughed as I explained to him that our structure and our ability to get things done were two entirely different things. We got things done because of relationship and trust and communication regardless of who reported to whom.

However, it would not be right to conclude that systems and clarity and clear responsibilities are wrong for a relay team or for a company. The bigger the company the greater the need for systems. But, if the systems block the exercise of relational collaboration the organization will suffer in the end.

Resistance to Innovation

Complexity Theory teaches that there are three states in which a system or organization may exist at any given time. *Chaos* is the lack of stability and clarity and direction; it is invariably destructive; cancer is a chaotic state for a body. *Stasis* is having so much stability and clarity and so many rules, policies and regulations that nothing can be done without umpteen signatures; stasis says, "We've never done it that way before" (aka, the Seven Last Words of a Dying Corporation). *Complexity* is the zone in which there are just enough rules to keep things moving forward but not so many as to stifle thought. It is in the moving target of complexity that all true innovation happens.

Larger companies are more prone to stasis than smaller ones. Consequently, they tend to be less innovative, less creative. More likely to copy than make disruptive change.

Lower Levels of Trust

I heard of someone who remarked in a meeting recently that they trusted their leader but that they didn't trust the company. Interesting. And revealing. The further we are away from the people making decisions the less relationship we have with them; the less relationship we have with leaders the less we trust them. It makes sense.

Ask Americans whether they trust their government and the overwhelming majority will say, "No." Their place on the political spectrum doesn't matter. Government is too big to engender trust. Or think about anything with "big" in front of it—*big* oil, *big* business, *big* bank, etc. The very terms themselves speak of lack of trust.

Large companies struggle to create environments of trust. It is not impossible but it is much more difficult than in a smaller company. The overuse of technology, such as email, contributes to this problem.

Employee Thinking vs. Owner Thinking

When colleagues begin to speak of *the* company instead of *my* company, there is a problem. That is when people think in terms of hours and PTO and benefits instead of the mission and the cause and their community.

Employees show up for work. They punch in; they punch out. They watch the clock. They maximize whatever is in it for them. They do enough but rarely do the extraordinary.

Owners, on the other hand, show up for work…sick. The clock is irrelevant to them except as it pertains to the promise made to a customer. They do whatever they can, not merely what they must. They treat equipment and money as if it were their own.

How many times have you done business with a large company and their representative, be they store clerk, checkout person, gate agent, or "customer service representative" only to be insulted and put off by their lack of true interest in you or the quality of their service to you. I remember having a dispute with AT&T over a fraudulent charge. As I escalated the issue through ranks I was amazed at how perfunctory and uncaring (yet polite) the response was. The straw finally broke the camel's back when a supervisor said, "Well sir, AT& T *feels*…" I immediately cut her off and said, "Ma'am, let's get one thing clear. AT&T doesn't *feel* anything. You feel things. I feel things. But AT&T doesn't."

The feeling of ownership that employees and colleagues have is a priceless asset for any company. It is rare in large companies and a peril of bigness.

Conclusion

You might think, as you read this that I am jaded against large companies. I'm not. However, it would be dishonest to not face some of the problems that accompany bigness. They are, as we say, reality.

Being Big and Yet Small

PART TWO

The Problem of Smallness

"Desire for security keeps littleness little and threatens the great with smallness."
--Anonymous

Another fun movie about size (great for the whole family) is *Honey, I Shrunk the Kids*. Rick Moranis plays a scientist whose children accidentally activate one of his inventions and end up being shrunk to the size of bugs. It's a great adventure but, at times, very dangerous as the children find themselves hunted by giant ants and other insects in their own backyard.

Being big has its problems. So, does being small. Most of us have worked for small companies (or small-minded companies) and we can easily recount the issues and challenges that can make little also undesirable.

Lack of Resources

Perhaps the most obvious of problems small companies face is that they simply don't have all the resources to do what they need to or to compete effectively with larger firms. We've all lived this at one time or another.

Internally, a small company may not have the compensation plan or benefits needed to recruit and retain top talent. Training is often "sit with Sally" or "on the job" or simply non-existent. I remember one small company with which I consulted where the new-hire sales training consisted of, "Here's the phone book. Here's the phone. Good luck." No wonder their turnover was 180%!

Legal help. HR expertise. Risk management. Sales management. Marketing materials. So many things are a struggle for the small company just in terms of equipping their colleagues to win.

And externally, this lack of resources can be crippling. When a client needs a product or service outside of the norm, the small company finds itself saying, "Sorry, we can't help you"

Too Many Hats

Because there are not enough resources and not enough people to do all that must be done, small companies resort, out of necessity, to having folks wear many hats and fill many roles. HR and Legal and Risk are one person. Payroll and Collections are one person. Managers are asked to say grace over everything in the field and have no backup.

A sure way to fail is to try to do too many things or too many different kinds of things at once. Yet, small companies face this challenge constantly. There are no fewer things or kinds of things to be done than in a large company; they just have fewer people and therefore those fewer people burn themselves out trying to be all things to all people.

Lack of Presence

You simply can't be everywhere. You can only stretch so far. This has two big applications.

First, you can't service clients in multiple locations simply because you don't have a location or a team in that particular geography. Not all clients demand that you service them everywhere but not having the ability to service them in most places is a huge weakness for small companies and, in some ways, helps keep them small. Many small business owners lament this Catch 22.

Second, you can't be with two clients at once. What happens to the small firm when ABC Company wants you to attend a vital production planning meeting and XYZ Company has their Global VP visiting and want you there? The answer is one client gets put off and you feel like a failure.

Small Town Thinking

If you've ever moved into a small town you know exactly what I mean when I use the term "provincial thinking." It comes out in various ways. Strange looks.

Extreme caution before friendship and trust is offered—all while being friendly and polite. In the Deep South, we tease about the question, "You ain't from around here are ya?" Every region of the country has the same question; it just comes out differently.

In small companies, this provincial thinking takes the form of the "Not Invented Here" (NIH) syndrome. New ideas are seen as meddling or being critical. People don't want to hear how you did it at your old company because it makes them feel inferior.

Small town thinking also demonstrates itself in the incredible difficulty a new team member has in just being accepted and fitting in. The absorption period can be months, years, or never even end if you weren't "there at the beginning."

The results of this mindset are that new ideas don't get shared, employee engagement is never fully realized, and the small company never fully realizes the ROI from new employees. Turnover increases. Productivity freezes or decreases.

Inadequate Technology

Unless the small company is a high-tech firm the odds are that small company's technology is simply insufficient to the task. Often technology is outdated, not universally available, delivered without training, or non-existent.

It's hard to grow in today's world without cutting edge or at least current technology. All companies face this challenge but especially small companies.

Conclusion

So, like big companies, small companies have their own problems. It's not realistic at all to think that everything is universal bliss in a small firm.

Being Big and Yet Small

PART THREE

The Desirability of Smallness

"Every small business will give you an entrepreneurial way of looking at things. I guarantee you that for every plant that closes, if you gave it to one small-business person in that community, he or she would find a way to make it work. The small-business attitude is you always find a way to make it work."
   --Hamdi Ulukaya

Many people long for the "good old days," usually forgetting that there was plenty about those days that was anything but good. Nevertheless, there are things about smallness — small towns, small stores, small companies — that are very attractive and very positive.

Belonging

We are all familiar with Maslow's Hierarchy of Needs:

Self-Actualization

Self-Esteem

Belonging

Security

Survival

The basic premise Maslow was trying to demonstrate is

that humans cannot achieve the highest levels of existence such as having a healthy self-esteem and self-actualization until their lower needs are met: food and shelter, basic safety, and a sense of belonging to a group in which they are cared for, i.e., belonging.

Note the particularly important place that belonging has in the upward journey. It is the bridge between barely living and fully living. This belonging or connectedness is a powerful part of being from a small town or working in a smaller company. People know each other. They know each other's families, habits, interests, abilities and liabilities. They are a village or tribe (as anthropologists would put it) and together they work hard to survive, to thrive and to find meaning.

Many small companies are characterized by a high degree of trust and interdependence that employees find satisfying and that brings a strong sense of safety. Trust, the confidence to stand with your back to your colleagues while you fend off attacks from outside or charge at the competition, is vital to human welfare and to sustainable company success. Who wouldn't want this?

Resourcefulness

Some of the greatest breakthroughs in life and business and technology have come, not because people were well supplied or well resourced, but because they were not! It was the lack of resources that led Toyota and Taichi Ohno to create the Toyota Production System (known in the U.S. as lean manufacturing). It was the lack of military hardware that led Israel to develop of one of the smallest yet most effective militaries in the world.

Necessity is the mother of invention. It is need that unleashes creativity and innovation not usually seen in more affluent companies. Doing more with less. Breakthrough technologies and work methodologies often come, not from resources but from resourcefulness. When you must figure things out, you do. When you must meet customer demands with less available to you than the competition you simply do it.

I think of the oxygen scrubber literally created from spare parts and duct tape in Houston that helped save the crew of Apollo 13 from certain death. I think of Jonas Salk testing the polio vaccine on himself and his family to save millions. I think of the men of the 101st Airborne who withstood the Nazi onslaught in Battle of the Bulge in December 1944 without winter gear and barely enough ammunition.

And resourcefulness is fun. It's energizing. The sheer hunger to succeed combined with fierce creativity is an exciting experience.

Cooperation

Necessity is the mother of invention; it is also the driver of cooperation. If we are short of funds or technology or headcount then we learn to work together. We find very quickly that the whole is greater than the sum of the parts and that synergy is more than a word that consultants use.

If you've ever had the experience of having to get something done, something that was of great importance, and you did it by joining up with a small handful of co-workers then you know how exhilarating this can be. It's the David and Goliath story for a team. It's the "band of brothers" experience. (Shakespeare, Henry V, Act IV, Scene iii).

Small companies typically have lots of these experiences and stories. They survive by working together and by depending on each other. They really don't have a choice.

Human Connection

When you walk through a large airport like Atlanta or Chicago's O'Hare or LAX or Heathrow, how at home do you feel? What kind of human connections do you make?

Large companies can feel like this. Small companies, on the other hand, are places where you actually know each other. You know the faces. You greet one another. You touch each other's lives.

Conclusion

So, there are many powerful and good things about small companies. These make working in them very attractive and fulfilling.

Being Big and Yet Small

PART FOUR

The Desirability of Bigness

"I'm a capitalist. I'm a CEO. I run a big business. I'm an employer."
--Sophia Amoruso

It is very easy to be critical of "big, bureaucratic, multi-layered" companies. They are often referred to as dinosaurs or, in the words of James Belasco, "elephants." However, it would be short-sighted to camp on the shortcomings of big companies just as it would be to stay focused on the shortcomings of small companies. Being big has some real and powerful benefits.

Resources and Scale

There is something to be said for being the "big kid." One of those things is that you have the resources to do things that small companies only dream of. Training and employee development is usually much stronger and more sophisticated in a large firm. Programs, compensation, special projects abound in the bigger company.

Perhaps the greatest resources that a big company brings to the table is money and people. How many times does a small company simply not have the financial strength to invest in a great idea or to take a big chance or to weather economic turbulence? The lack of investment capital stymies expansion, technology, innovation, and the ability to bring powerful solutions to clients. Stated positively, there are so many things you can do because simply because you are large and have the funds to do them.

People are even more vital than cash. With the human capital, the talent to do things, things get done. Project teams are formed. Task forces are created. Skunk works are held. People—in terms of sheer numbers and raw ability—are abundant in a large company and that is a decided advantage in building a great place to work and a great provider of services.

In our search for "closeness," we often forget that much of that came around the table of want and lack. Big means resources to do more.

Reinforcements and Redundant Systems

We usually think of redundant as unnecessary. However, it can also mean backups and safety.

On an airplane, redundant systems mean that if one set of controls fails, there is a backup or redundant set to kick in.

In the military, reinforcements are the reserve troops that are sent in when the main force is either in trouble on or in need of a bit more power to finish the battle. It's not that different in a company.

Redundancy and backups mean that when technology fails there are alternatives and workarounds while dedicated resources fix the problem. Reinforcement means that we can offer payment terms to our customers because we have the reserves and credit to do so. Buffer systems mean a large company can take people off their job to train them and yet the job gets done or that colleagues can take a vacation or be sick. It means there is more than one person to ask for assistance or guidance on legal, risk, computer systems, sales or any other issue that arises. Reinforcement means there are teams to help implement big projects, launch new client sites, etc.

Negotiating Power

If the hubbub about U.S. healthcare for the last 8 years has taught us anything it has taught us that healthcare is expensive—very expensive. Yet, a large company, because of its size and colleague population can negotiate a much more affordable program for employees than a small one. When you're big you can ask more and you will usually get more—discounts on car rentals or office supplies to name a couple of items.

The real negotiating power, though, is in dealing with clients and prospects. A company with powerful programs, multiple locations, impactful client solution can demand and get a better price, better margin, better terms for the services rendered and, at the same time, because of lower costs of doing business, generate better profit.

The one rule of negotiating that always works is to negotiate from strength. To negotiate from weakness is practically begging. It's when you can bring more to the table and afford to walk away from the table that you can bring about true win-win results.

Presence

The very last thing you want to say to a prospect is, "Sorry, but we can't help you with that" or "We're not in Dallas." Walmart wins because it's big and because it is practically everywhere. Even towns without stoplights have a Walmart.

The incredible power of being able to tell someone, "Yes, we can help you there and in 500 other locations" is amazing. It's more than just bragging rights. It's about the ability to make a difference, to serve people, to serve clients wherever they need it. From New York City to Paris, Alabama to Los Angeles, São Paulo to Sydney, you can say, "Yes!"

Presence is more than just geography. It is also being able to bring a universe of solutions, of answers to customers. To be big enables a company to more accurately say, "Wherever you are, we are there. Whatever you need, we can bring it to you."

Living Outside the Comfort Zone

No pain, no gain. No discomfort, no learning. No learning, no personal growth. The reality is that for many people working in a big company, especially when they came from a small one or when they grew from small to big, brings great discomfort and uncertainty.

Let's face it. You don't always know who to call. You may have to have another signature on something. Things may take a bit longer at times. You may be asked to expand our role or take on a different role entirely. All of this is uncomfortable.

But stated positively, these things stretch us, expand our horizons, expose us to new things, force us to use muscles and abilities that had lain dormant. This is healthy. This is good for us. When I exercise I rarely enjoy the moment but my body is stronger and my mind is clearer as a result.

Think of your life. When were your periods of greatest personal growth? In times of ease? I doubt it. If you're like me you grew the most when things were the toughest.

Technology

Unless you're in a high-tech startup the odds are that the big company technology (overall) is superior to that of a small company. Whether it is having laptops for all employees or VOIP or video conferencing or any number of technologies, these things make business better and they tend to be found, or at least are more plentiful and readily available, in a big company.

I maintain that people and cash are the two greatest assets any company can bring to the market. Right behind these, however, is technology. It may be a "business accelerator" (per Jim Collins) or it may be an industry disruptor (like the iPhone). Either way, if you have the capital, the talent, and the toys you are probably going to win in the long run.

Employee Opportunities

In my time with my company as we've grown from small to big to the biggest of our kind, I've had a dozen different titles (so many that I simply don't put them on my business card anymore) and the chance to do things that could fill up multiple careers. My LinkedIn profile is almost impossible to understand because of all the roles I've had the privilege of filling.

A big company simply has more career opportunities for its employees. You can move to a new city. You can be promoted to a new position. Move laterally to take on a different challenge or execute a personal passion. There is almost no end to what you can be if you, first, fill the space that you are in, and, second, never stop learning.

Conclusion

Not everything about being big is desirable. Not everything is undesirable either. To focus on the positive, to find the good, to leverage the opportunity of being big is the key to thriving in your new, bigger company!

Being Big and Yet Small

PART FIVE

The Best of Both Worlds

"It might be said now that I have the best of both worlds. A Harvard education and a Yale degree."
--John F. Kennedy

Let me begin this section by stating unequivocally that it is possible to be big and small at the same time. It's a "both/and" scenario in which we have two individual

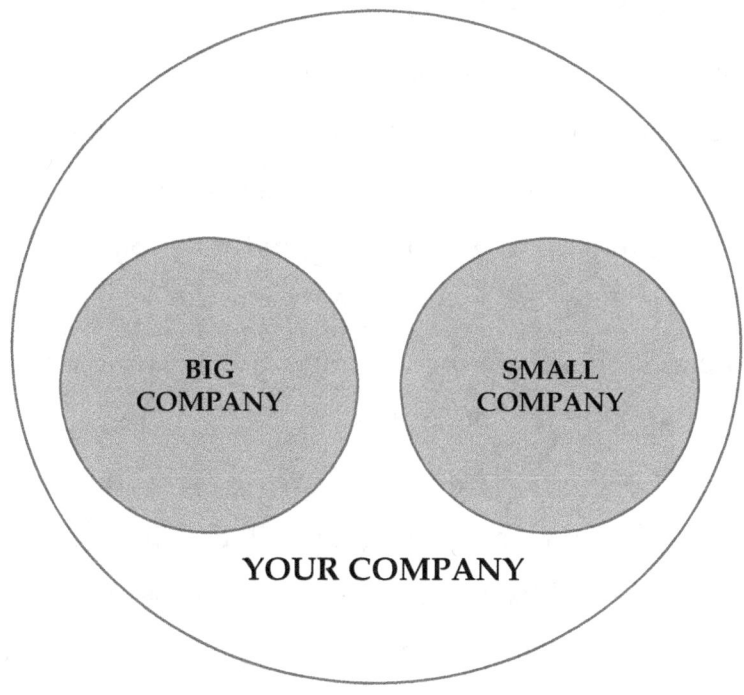

circles—big and small—and we simply draw another circle around them both. This is what I call the "best of both worlds." In other words, it is entirely possible to capture the best parts of a small company and the best parts of a big company and build them all into *your* company.

The next few chapters will outline some specific ways that your company can capture the "best of both worlds" and leave your trepidation behind. This chapter will focus on a few more general principles to embrace to help you get there.

Believe

Sometimes I end up in conversations with someone who, no matter what, has decided to hold a particular view regardless of reality. This happens in politics, for example. It also happens in organizational development. If someone simply doesn't like being small or big and is determined to hold onto that opinion then they will. You can save your breath, avoid arguments, and hope they can find a company where they will be happy.

On the other hand, if you determine that it can work and that you want it to work and that you will look for the positive, the best will usually happen. Don't confuse me with Pollyanna. I'm not saying everything is good. Everything is not good and never will be. Big or small. Yet, your attitude contributes so much to your experience that we need to give it special attention.

Essentialism

In his excellent book, *Essentialism,* Greg McKeown outlines how to get the clutter out of our lives and bring focus to what matters the most, what he terms *the vital few.* The idea is that amid all the things you *could* do, there are only a few things you *should* do. Do you know what those are? Does your company know what those are? Knowing and acting on this principle is key to thriving in a big company.

There is a powerful scene in *Moscow on the Hudson* in which Robin Williams, who plays a Russian musician who defected to the U.S., volunteers to run an errand for his hosts and pick up coffee at the local grocer. He panics when he is on the coffee aisle. The sheer number of choices (something not known in the U.S.S.R) is overwhelming and sends him into an anxiety attack and hyper-ventilation. It's easy to feel like Robin Williams' character when there is so much to think about. So many people. So many locations. So many departments. So many changes.

The answer is to stop. Get your bearings. Return to what matters the most: your core values and mission and the vital few things you need to do. Don't let the clamor confuse you. Don't let others drag you into their drama. Don't let the crowd panic you. Pick your course and go after that as if you had blinders on.

Leadership Development at All Levels

Leadership is not about a position or a title or power. Leadership is for everyone regardless of where you fit in the organization. Leadership is the ability to influence others to do what should be done and to go where they need to go — without the power to make them do it. It's about winning hearts and minds. It's about impacting people's "want to."

Years ago, when I led a franchise turnaround, I told my team that if we ever had to pull the contract out to get something done with a franchise owner then we had already lost the battle. Our job was to figure out the best path and enable others to see it and want to take it. After growing that division by a factor of 6X in just three years we proved the point. The same thing is true in family, in friendships, and in business — if you can't persuade with truth and caring, then bringing out your hammer is a failure.

Because everyone can lead and should lead that means that one of your biggest tasks is to invest in leadership development at every level of the company. It's not just for those whose title demands it. It's for everyone…period. Training, conferences, special projects, coaching and more are the ways you must and will do this.

A company filled with leaders will always capture the

best of both worlds.

Leaders Who Get Their Hands Dirty

A common trap for leaders in companies that become big is what I've heard called "executivitis." That's a fun term for the pride that begins to invade our self-concept when we start to believe that we are somehow bigger and better and more valuable than others. The logical (actually, illogical) outcome of this kind of thinking is expressed in the term "RHIP" or "rank has its privileges."

Reality is quite the opposite. True leaders serve. True leaders have humility. True leaders aren't above any task and aren't better than anyone else. They take on anything. They do what needs to be done. They say, "Follow me" instead of "Obey me." They lead by example. That's why I say they roll up their sleeves and get their hands dirty.

If you've ever worked for a "leader" who believed he or she was more important than the team, you I know exactly what I'm talking about. By the same token, if you've had the privilege of working for and with a true leader, a "level 5 leader" (to quote Jim Collins in *Good to Great*) you have a pretty good idea of what you need to be.

The Primacy of Relationships

The final general principle of embracing the best of

both big and small is to place relationships above all else. A family that puts work first will suffer. A company that puts anything over people will likewise be weak. The very term "company" comes from the Latin word for team, partner, and friend.

When a company recognizes the primacy of relationships, the foundation is laid for a powerful business and a powerful employment experience. It is realizing that every person in your company deserves to be spoken to with kindness and never degraded, to be considered in every decision as more than a statistic, to be listened to and heard, and to have input and voice in company matters. That is what can set you apart from other big companies. It is using things you learned in kindergarten like "please and thank you" that demonstrate respect for one another. It is in executing on commitments in a timely and transparent manner that shows you hold others in esteem and as worthy as yourself.

Show me a company that is truly characterized by committed and caring relationships and I will show you a company that can accomplish just about anything and to which colleagues will long to belong!

Conclusion

Focusing on the essential few things, being true servant-leaders, and building strong relationships of trust and honesty are what will make the difference. This will help you to be both big and small.

Being Big and Yet Small

PART SIX

The Fabric of Communication

"Communication leads to community."

--Rollo May

The essence of any company, of any community is communication. Anthropologically, a "people group" is defined as a group of people having a common language, similar geography, and linked culture. Language is the building block of all relationships. Language is what makes life work. Communication is vital.

Often, the first casualty of becoming big is communication. The old, proven channels of connecting and communicating break down. They cease to work as they once did and they are certainly not up to the task of carrying information and ideas throughout the new, larger organization. Many of us remember the old days of dial up internet and the screech that came from two modems connecting at the amazing speed of 56kbps. Emails barely got through, files almost never, and graphics? Well, you can forget graphics. In the same way, the old "modem speeds" of a once-small company cannot hope to transmit information fast enough or in enough volume to work in the new company. That's why you can always count on the complaint, "We don't know what's going on anymore!"

Smart, big companies do not dismiss this or accept this as normal. It's real and it's true but communications problems cannot be allowed to stand. We must find new, better, and faster means of connecting if we are to be successful.

Large Scale, Big Tent Communications

A common and somewhat effective method of communicating within a big company is what we can style "big tent" events. These are the meetings, conferences, conference calls, webcasts, video conferences, newsletters, intranets, etc. in which a very few presenters convey their ideas and messages to a very broad and large audience.

Big tent events do work, in *certain* ways. They offer a "one-on-many" venue for leadership and experts to set the tone, to share a common vision, to lay out a new strategy, to teach and to update. Granted that some presenters are more effective in this setting than others yet, overall, big tent events accomplish their purpose: the one-way transmission of data.

But, big tents are not the right place for two-way communication. They do not offer an effective or scalable way to interact, to exchange ideas, to debate, to adjust, to edit. No matter how many "toss around microphones," Q&A sessions, or high tech "tweet you questions" approaches you use, big tents are one way. Consequently, while information flows at a rapid rate to a large audience, learning and embrace and collaboration are relatively low. The overall return on investment of time and money is questionable at best and ineffective in times of rapid change. Certainly, they are not able to build strong communication alone.

Smaller Community Meetings

Since effective communication involves more than just broadcasting we must find other ways to make it work. There must be the two-way exchange of information, ideas, opinions and feelings. Adults process information interactively and only learn and change when they are able to do so. Enter the smaller meeting.

Management experts have long slammed meetings as inefficient, ineffective and wasteful of time and money. This is true if they are, like most of what we all see, poorly planned, poorly organized, and poorly led. Business magazines and comic strips are filled with jokes about how miserable most company meetings are. If we can learn to think of meetings correctly and to plan and execute them expertly then we will find them to be a powerful medium for interactive communication among the teams of people that comprise the company.

The purpose of this booklet and chapter is not to teach meeting management. Enough is available on that topic already. It is to say, though, that good meetings foster good communication and we should learn how to hold them.

Examples of smaller meetings that are needed (and I would argue they are more needed the bigger you get) include *geographical* gatherings like regions, areas, or branches. There are *functional* meetings in which people from different geographies but who have similar jobs and responsibilities communicate about skills and best practices and ideas germane to them alone. Meetings focused on a brand or product line make sense in this context. Task forces and special project team meetings are examples of meetings built around a shared purpose or task. In fact, any topic or behavior or identity that people have in common can be solid ground on which to meet effectively.

Some might ask, how small is small? Too small would be less than 2. Too big is more than 150 (based on average tribal and village sizes studied by anthropologists). For more insight on group sizes for optimum collaboration and communication see Simon Sinek's excellent book, *Leaders Eat Last*.

Utilize All Available Media

While there is a great need to make sure we use each medium as it was meant to be used (for example, emails were not intended to be forums for discussion or lengthy announcements), now it's more important to simply make sure that we use everything at our disposal to improve communication and, hence, connection of people to people. The tendency we have is to find a favorite medium (email or text) and use that to the exclusion of other media that would be more effective in a particular application. In other words, if the simplest way to communicate is to use the phone then pick it up and dial.

The technology at our disposal is almost endless. We have phones—still the fastest and best way to gain understanding or resolve disagreements other than in-person dialogue. We have email; even though we often abuse it, email can be very effective if used correctly. Social media can be harnessed within a company whether it be Facebook, Facebook Groups, Twitter or Yammer. Skype for Business used as Instant Messenger, voice meetings and/or video meetings is becoming easier to manage and very helpful. One under-utilized resource for effective communication is to establish a robust company intranet. Rather than making it the last place to go, turn it into your daily newspaper where you can get company news, industry headlines, video messages from leaders and much more. Go to Meeting type technologies (like Zoom or JoinMe) are stable and useful platforms. The old, reliable conference call can be extremely beneficial (especially, if you learn how to better plan, manage and execute them).

Probably by the time we publish this book a new medium will have come on the scene. Some of my early adopter colleagues are certainly lamenting the existing technology I failed to mention. Nevertheless, from drumbeats and smoke signals to fiber optic connectivity, every group of people has had to learn to communicate to survive, much less thrive.

A Word on Listening

In *The Seven Habits of Highly Effective People,* Steven Covey said, "Seek first to understand; then to be understood." There is great wisdom in that statement. We haven't truly communicated until we've increased understanding and we cannot understand if we don't listen.

I often imagine (and I know I'm not alone) what people are actually doing during conference calls (their nails, emails, reading the paper, playing with their dog, shopping on Amazon?). I wonder what is so all-fired important that you must be on your phone typing away as the CEO is outlining the new company direction? Or, where is my mind while you are talking to me—a million miles away or thinking of what I will say next?

People change only when they learn and understand. People learn and understand when they take the time to listen, really listen. It's hard. It's not natural even though it should be (given that we were created with two ears and only one mouth!).

A culture of communication is not just a culture of talking. It is a culture of interactive expression, listening, considering and changing. Perhaps each of us should make a point of going back in time and rereading the classic *How to Win Friends and Influence People* by Dale Carnegie.

Conclusion

Of all the things I've written so far, I cannot think of anything more important than excellence in communication when it comes to being big and yet small at the same time. The more you know, the more you understand and the more you are understood the more a part of this company you will feel and the smaller it will become to you…even as it grows larger!

Being Big and Yet Small

PART SEVEN
Tribes and Nations

"What tribes are, is a very simple concept that goes back 50 million years. It's about leading and connecting people and ideas. And it's something that people have wanted forever."
--Seth Godin

When I left home to attend the University of Tennessee (also known as God's Country), I was overwhelmed by the sheer number of students. This was in 1973 and very few universities had 35,000 students in those days; Texas, if I remember correctly, had 50,000; Michigan had a similar enrollment. To a boy from a high school with only 1700 students and only 350 in my graduating class this seemed like a giant ant hill and I was just one of the ants.

I noticed soon, however, how quickly the massive student body began to self-organize into smaller groups—fraternities, sororities, independents, students from this dorm, students from that dorm, intramural teams and so on. It was simple human nature at work. In the midst of a crowd, people will seek out a few others with whom they can connect and build deep relationships.

The Tribal Structure

Today, I live in the mountains of North Carolina where the original culture was Cherokee. My ancestry includes Choctaw and my wife's traces back to the Cherokee in our area. We hike these mountains and often think of what their life was like. It was, of course, rugged and focused on survival. It was, in many ways, communal. And it thrived in the wilderness. It was also tribal.

A tribe is a gathering of families and villages who see common cause with each other. Defense. Survival. Hunting. Marriage. Procreation. Virtually every part of North America was populated by tribes of indigenous people organized on this simple principle.

Tribes were also characterized by a common language, common history, common customs, common dress, and even common ancestry. There were some differences within the tribe but for the most part they were very similar and homogeneous.

Tribes or clans (as they are sometimes called) are universal, it turns out. You find this same structure in South Asia, Central Asia, Africa, indigenous Australia and New Zealand, ancient Israel, and, in a less identifiable way, in the Goths and Visigoths of Europe.

Tribalism didn't end with the American Indians. It's still very much alive. Just look at the passion around NCAA football or basketball. Visit a Steelers' Fan Club bar. There is a powerful identity that comes from being a fan (short for fanatic) and it helps to hold society together.

It's also very much alive in companies…in your company. You have regions, brands, areas, front office, back office, sales, manufacturing, logistics. These are tribes in a very real sense. One of them is your tribe. And this isn't bad at all. It's how we cope with huge populations in schools, companies, cities and nations. It's only bad when one tribe goes to war with another or refuses to acknowledge the worth of another.

And so, enter the…

Nations

Within Native American culture and the tribal structure there were larger collections of tribes into what were known as "nations." There was the Cherokee Nation, the Sioux Nation, the Apache Nation, the Navajo Nation. Nations weren't just large tribes. They weren't metropolitan centers. They were all the tribes who shared a language, history, customs and cause, who recognized their need for the other tribes within their "nation."

A Sioux who killed another Sioux was considered a

murderer. A Sioux who killed a Mohican, on the other hand, would be a hero. The nation was comprised of the tribes and other nations were comprised of other tribes. They were larger units made up of smaller units.

There might be some differences within a nation — dialect, geography, preferred food, mating customs, for example. But they still saw themselves as being united.

That's where the big company comes in. Within your company there are many tribes, as we've seen. They are identifiable and important to success. Yet, you are *one company, one nation*.

Do we have differences between the various tribes? Sure. You use different terms for things like titles or forms or products. You live and work in different places. You have different heritages. Yet, you are one. You are voluntarily united in one large organization that recognizes that each member and each member tribe needs the rest. To not recognize this is like killing a member of the nation. In business terms, the competition is "out there" and not "in here."

Living Tribally and Nationally

So, what does this mean in practical terms to you and how does this help your company be big and small? I suggest several important things…

First, never refer to yourselves as anything other than the nation—you are YOUR COMPANY. There are no legacy people. There are only people in *your* nation.

Do you remember September 11, 2001? I do. America pulled together as it never has in my lifetime. That day, I called my Dad, a highly decorated WWII hero, and asked him, "Is this how it felt when Pearl Harbor was attacked?" He replied, "Exactly." United. Focused. One nation!

Second, respect the value and contribution each tribe within the nation makes. Revenue doesn't have a regional flavor. EBITDA smells the same in every brand and division. Front office can't survive without back office, sales can't survive without manufacturing. Every part, every tribe is necessary to the health of the nation, the company.

Third, celebrate your own tribes. Tribes exist to give people a place to belong. Remember Maslow's Hierarchy and how important that sense of belonging is. I have a team. I have a place. It's my team. Its members are my teammates. That's a special relationship and a big part of how your make *big* seem *small*. Work to make your tribe excellent, focused, sticky, and inclusive.

Conclusion

Does the tribal analogy seem silly? Perhaps it is but it's human nature and there are thousands of years of history on my side. A company is not a bunch of individual contributors. You and I are part of a tribe and department, part of a gathering of tribes and regions, and we are a nation, *one company.*

PART EIGHT

The Enemy is Not the Future...It's the Past

"Nostalgia often leads to idle speculation."

--J. Paul Getty

Definition of nostalgia

1. **1:** *the state of being homesick:* homesickness
2. **2:** *a wistful or excessively sentimental yearning for return to or of some past period or irrecoverable condition; also: something that evokes nostalgia*
--Merriam-Webster

I'm betting you can see the problem already. Nostalgia is not just longing for your high school athletic victories or being homesick for your birthplace or missing your puppy from when you were little. It can also be looking back on being small, on the way things used to be with a wistfulness and even a kind of mourning. And it can be very unhealthy.

Have you ever stopped to consider that when you are nostalgic, your memories are almost always pleasant? Things were just better back then. The good ol' days were good. Nostalgia is about how good it was.

I hate to burst your bubble but it wasn't all good.

Being Big and Yet Small

Nostalgia is wrong! In high school, you may have won the big game but you also had horrible acne. Your birthplace was actually a dump. Your puppy bit you. Your cat peed on your pillow. There was conflict in the company when we were little. Somehow, we forget this part of the past and create a sort of *faux past.* A past that wasn't real.

The Problems with the Living in the Past

If we insist on living in the past we are consigning ourselves to a series of problems, many of which we may not even be aware. After all, our memories are good.

First of all, the past is past. It's gone. It can't be relived. It can't be repeated. It was. It isn't now. It was. No matter how hard I try, I can't get my hair back. No matter how hard we wish, we aren't the small companies we once were. Things will never be as they were; they can't be.

Secondly, a more nefarious problem with living in the past is that it biases you toward the present. Falsely happy memories of what used to be cast a dark shadow over the things that are now. It's never quite like it used to be. The meetings aren't as good as they used to be. The communications aren't as clear. Relationships aren't as close. Income isn't as robust. Advancement isn't as rapid.

The comparisons of now to then and of today to yesterday, usually built on nostalgic inaccuracies, are dangerous. They lead to unhappiness, dissatisfaction, disappointment and disillusionment. I've never known a person who lives in the past to be engaged in, much less abandoned to, the work at hand.

If you want to enjoy today then learn to put yesterday behind you. I'm not suggesting that you never enjoy memories—nothing of the sort. But if they block your embrace of today then set them aside and put them in their proper place.

Thirdly, nostalgia cheats you out of the future. The past may seem "secure" because it actually happened. The future is "insecure" and uncertain. It hasn't happened yet. But one thing is certain. If we insist on living in the past and clinging to the way we were we will never have eyes to see what may yet be.

Signs of Living in the Past

How do you know if you're living in the past, clinging to what was instead of living in the now and adventuring into the future? Here are several signs that you should watch out for.

If you find yourself critical of everything (or most things or even many things) it may be because you are living in the past. We've already touched on this but if it was so good then, when it likely wasn't, then it can't be better today.

Critical spirits dominate individuals, teams and companies longing for what used to be. The leadership just isn't quite with it. We can't believe they said what they said. People think other people dress "unprofessionally" or, on the other hand, like "stuffed shirts." Silly stuff, mostly.

Phrases like, "We used to do it this way" and "Do You remember those meetings?" pepper the landscape. After meetings folks compare decisions and style and results with a negative tone. In fact, comparisons are almost constant and seemingly unconscious.

Factions and cliques are also signs of living in the past. Not venturing out beyond the circles in which you have always been comfortable (at least according to your faulty memories) keep you from circulating and blending the talents with which the new larger company has been blessed. Divisions, sides, legacies — all these are evidence of living in the past and of corporate nostalgia.

How do you stack up? Is your company nostalgic? Are you trapped in the past and comparing everything to "then?"

Moving Forward

Let me make it clear that I am not trying to show disdain for the past. I have a past. You have a past. We have a past. There were many great things in the past. When the company was small things were good…sometimes. There was a lot to enjoy and a lot to be thankful for. I am making a case for letting the past be the past and moving on.

But how?

Let me suggest that the first thing to do is to make two key acknowledgements. The past had some great moments and great accomplishments, a lot of laughter and fun. And, the past had a lot of problems. Lots of pain, frustration, anger, conflict and failures. True? If you say, "Yes," then you've just made a major step toward living now. A realistic appraisal of what used to be is the great liberator from nostalgia.

See the opportunities all around you. That's next. Today, you have opportunities to do new things, to develop new solutions, to create new technology, to change more lives. They are right here and right now. A chance to do things never done before. But you must see it! You and your team must open your eyes and look to your right and left and see what is there. It wasn't there back then. You couldn't do it back then.

Embrace the learning right in front of you. That's the third thing. I can say, for my part, the last few years (my company went through a multi-billion dollar merger) have been like learning in hyper-space. Can you say that? We've seen new things and done new things and gone new places. It's everywhere and you can't have it if you live in yesteryear. Sometimes I feel as if I've earned ten MBAs in the last 24 months! How cool is that?

Finally, make great, new friends. Everyone in the new, big company has the chance to make great, new friends. Coworkers tend to become friends if you let them. If there's no room in your heart for new people then you are in for a rough ride. However, if your heart and mind are open to add to your circles of friends then your lives can only be richer.

Conclusion

I've visited many retirement homes in my time and I've noticed two kinds of people there. There are those who are morose and sad, always longing for what used to be and who they used to be with. Critical and lonely people. But, I've also met others who were energetic despite their infirmity, joyful despite their life-losses, and socially connected to others around them even though they miss their family. This group lives today…now…in the present.

I suspect companies are much the same. Morose and unhappy employees living in a company that no longer exists. Engaged and excited employees building a company that is now and will continue to be in the future.

Which will you be?

PART NINE

The Core Values are Core

It's the job of any business owner to be clear about the company's nonnegotiable core values. They're the riverbanks that help guide us as we refine and improve on performance and excellence. A lack of riverbanks creates estuaries and cloudy waters that are confusing to navigate. I want a crystal-clear, swiftly flowing stream.
--Danny Meyer

A home is no more stable than its foundation. A skyscraper can stand because it's pilings go deep into the earth to find bedrock. An ocean liner can stay upright because of the weight and depth of its keel. And a company can be big and yet small if it has and maintains a deep commitment to a simple set of shared values.

In *Built to Last,* Jim Collins presents his research on why certain companies stand the test of time, why decades after their founding leaders have passed on these companies remain strong and steady. One of his key findings is what he termed "Core Ideology," i.e., that each lasting company had taken the time to identify, codify and institutionalize a set of core beliefs, core values.

Many companies have core values. The dividing line is whether they choose to live them or not. I believe that this question is a powerful answer to how you can be both big and small.

Hire to the Values

There is nothing advantageous about bringing someone into the company who does not already share your corporate values. You cannot teach honesty. You cannot teach passion. You cannot teach caring. You either have it or you don't. As one person said, "Hire attitude; teach skills." Not the other way around!

Fire to the Values

I have often told audiences that there are two ways to lose your job in a great company. The first is long-term, sustained failure to perform. The numbers tell the story and termination in such a case comes as no surprise.

The other is to bust a core value. Now I don't mean to slip, to be human, or to fail. We all do that. I do mean to knowingly, deliberately and egregiously violate a fundamental belief like integrity or honesty. At that point, the violator needs to go for the sake of the whole.

Promote to the Values

Just being in a position for a long time does not qualify someone for the next role. Nor does doing a good job. Both are important but if a person is struggling to live the basic beliefs the team or company share as foundational then they are simply not ready for promotion.

Institutionalize the Values

You must be sure that your values outlive their authors in much the same way that, as a country, America must ensure that our Constitution outlives the Founding Fathers. You must memorialize the values with stories, visual cues, and so forth to make sure that those who come after you know and embrace the why, how and what of the company. You are, my friends, building something to last, something that is bigger than you.

Honor the Values

What is rewarded gets repeated. That's an inviolable law of human nature. If cheaters prosper then cheating will increase. If character is recognized then it will be strengthened. That's why it's so important that we praise and recognize those who live the company values, who do things that demonstrate the values and that prove the power of the culture in real life.

Conclusion

Values know no scale. Belief is greater than small or big. If your company has and holds a shared philosophy, if you build on this and strengthen this and reinforce this, you will be a great company that knows how to be big and still small.

CONCLUSION

I'll end where I started. Your company is big. It doesn't matter how or why you got here. You are here. You are a big company.

Some people love being big. Some people are very uncomfortable being big. Most are probably indifferent to it overall.

There are great advantages of being big. There are great advantages of being small. There are difficulties being small just as there are being big.

The challenge is to find the best of all worlds and optimize them in your company. It's what I call being big and small at the same time. I believe it can be done. I believe it must be done. And I believe it will be done.

If…you work together to make it so.

Being Big and Yet Small

ABOUT THE AUTHOR

Michael Baer has a background that looks like multiple careers. He is an entrepreneur. He was a pastor for 15 years. He has run construction companies, consulting companies and is an in-demand strategic coach. He is also an international speaker, teacher and incubator of businesses (especially among the ultra-poor of the 4th World).

Today, Michael is the Chief Development Officer of EmployBridge, the largest industrial staffing company in North America, the Executive Director of International Micro Enterprise Development, and an active investor/advisor to small businesses such as WeDo Worldwide, and Avoda International.

Michael and his wife live in the mountains of North Carolina where she operates her award-winning Bed and Breakfast, the *Elizabeth Leigh Inn*. They enjoy hiking and especially their incredible grandchildren.

Michael is a graduate of Flagler College and Dallas Theological Seminary.

www.ingramcontent.com/pod-product-compliance
Lightning Source LLC
Chambersburg PA
CBHW050016230526
45470CB00003B/992